40TH NEW YORK INFANTRY MONUMENT, Gettysburg National Military Park, Pennsylvania

UNION ZOUAVE

Published by Thomasson-Grant, Inc., Frank L. Thomasson III and John F. Grant, Directors;
C. Douglas Elliott, Product Development; Megan R. Youngquist, Art Director;
Carolyn M. Clark, Senior Editor; Jim Gibson, Production Manager.
Designed by Leonard G. Phillips
Edited by Elizabeth L.T. Brown
Photography by Sam Abell
Text by Brian C. Pohanka

Color separations by Pioneer Graphic through CGI (Malaysia) Sdn. Bhd.
Printed and bound in Japan by Dai Nippon Printing Co., Ltd.

95 94 93 92 91 90 89   5 4 3 2

Any inquiries should be directed to Thomasson-Grant, Inc.,
One Morton Drive, Suite 500, Charlottesville, Virginia 22901, telephone (804) 977-1780.

Library of Congress Cataloging-in-Publication Data

Pohanka, Brian.
   Distant thunder.

   1. United States—History—Civil War, 1861-1865—
Pictorial works.   I. Abell, Sam.   II. Title.
E468.7.P64   1988   973.7'022'2   88-40169
ISBN 0-934738-35-1

DISTANT THUNDER

A PHOTOGRAPHIC ESSAY ON THE AMERICAN CIVIL WAR

PHOTOGRAPHY BY SAM ABELL

TEXT BY BRIAN C. POHANKA

THOMASSON-GRANT
Charlottesville, Virginia

CIVIL WAR MONUMENT, Bethel, Maine

DEPENDING UPON POLITICS, it was called "The War of the Rebellion" or "The War of Northern Aggression." Historians have termed it "The Needless War," "The Irrepressible Conflict," and "The American Iliad." Whatever its nomenclature, the American Civil War profoundly affected our country's history. One hundred and twenty-five years later, we still feel its social and political repercussions and seek to come to terms with its underlying causes.

Government statistics tell us that the average Union soldier was a 25-year-old farmer with brown hair, blue eyes, and a light complexion; he stood 5 feet 8¼ inches tall and weighed 143½ pounds. Comparable figures do not exist for the Confederate forces, but it is safe to assume that the typical Southern volunteer resembled his Northern counterpart. While the existence of slavery may have been the conflict's single most important cause, the average soldier was neither an abolitionist nor a slave-holder. Most Northerners fought to preserve the Union, and most Southerners fought to preserve the political integrity of their respective states. Both sides fought to maintain what they saw as the most fundamental ideals of the nation's Founding Fathers. Be they Union or Confederate, the volunteers who marched to war in the spring of 1861 believed that their cause was right.

"I am willing to peril life for the welfare of our brave soldiers and in our country's cause," wrote Chaplain Arthur Buckminster Fuller of the 16th Massachusetts. "If God requires that sacrifice of me, it shall be offered on the altar of freedom, and in defense of all that is good in American institutions." Confederate Major William McKim expressed a similarly firm conviction that his side was battling "for the sacred right of self-government...in vindication of the principles enunciated in the Declaration of Independence."

The intensity with which these men fought was also fueled by an increasingly deadly arsenal. The iron fragments of artillery shells and the iron balls of canister that spewed from cannon like giant shotgun blasts mangled bodies beyond recognition. Limbs shattered by .58-caliber bullets were usually amputated; soldiers who survived the operation were likely to die of gangrene or tetanus. Hand-to-hand combat with 18-inch steel bayonets, musket butts, knives, rocks, and bare hands was not uncommon.

The carnage of Civil War battlefields still shocks. More than 620,000 men were killed in battle or died from wounds and disease. Some 470,000 others were injured, many of them crippled for life. More American soldiers fell in a single day of fighting at Antietam than in the entire campaign for Iwo Jima in World War II. Yet despite the war's savagery, its soldiers never quite lost their idealism; instead, they struggled to maintain their decorum in a way that seems almost incomprehensible from our 20th-century perspective.

CONFEDERATE PRIVATE

They were, after all, Victorians. Theirs was a rigidly structured society of solid institutions, firmly rooted values, and strictly defined codes of conduct. It was an age in which duty and honor were believed to be soldierly virtues, not propagandistic clichés. War was considered a splendid arena for glorious deeds. "There was a dash of chivalric romance in the social life during those days," Susan Leigh Blackford, the wife of a Confederate officer, recalled. "It was the legitimate outcome of nature that there should be a heroine for every hero." A month before he died in battle, Union General George Bayard reminded his father, "Honor and glory are before me — shame lurks in the rear."

Civil War history abounds with stirring declamations and flamboyant gestures. Union General George Custer and Confederate General Tom Rosser exchanged salutes before the Battle of Toms Brook, each "like a gartered knight in the lists." Mark Kerns, a mortally wounded Union artillery captain, told his assailants, "I promised to drive you back or die under my guns, and I have kept my word." The dying Union General James Rice ordered the surgeon who amputated his leg to "turn my face to the enemy." Soldiers of the 5th Connecticut sang "Rally Round the Flag, Boys" at the height of the Battle of Resaca, and North Carolinians chorused "The Bonnie Blue Flag" amidst the carnage of Spotsylvania. As he prepared to lead his brigade in a suicidal charge on Kennesaw Mountain, Union Colonel Daniel McCook took time to regale the troops with Thomas Macaulay's paean to the Roman hero Horatius:

> Then out spake brave Horatius,
> The Captain of the Gate:
> "To every man upon this earth
> Death cometh soon or late.
> And how can man die better
> Than facing fearful odds,
> For the ashes of his fathers
> And the temples of his Gods."

Civil War battles were replete with all the pomp of 19th-century warfare. The parade-ground precision with which Union troops deployed and advanced through a blizzard of Confederate shellfire at the Battle of Fredericksburg, methodically closing gaps torn through their ranks, caused Robert E. Lee to exclaim, "It is well that war is so terrible — we should grow too fond of it!"

Regiments were usually arrayed in a two-rank line of battle, the men standing elbow to elbow, regimental flags in the center of the line, field officers on horseback behind it. Although skirmishers in front of the main line of battle had permission to use cover, and some sharpshooter units wore green uniforms as camouflage, many more regiments sported the gaudy red and blue of the French Zouaves, and concealment was generally of slight concern to commanders.

FORT JEFFERSON, Florida

Little changed since Napoleon's time, the tactics of mid-19th-century warfare were founded on close-order formations of men expected to smash through the enemy's line with massive volleys of musketry. Confederate General William Taliaferro described one such clash at the Battle of Brawner's Farm on August 28, 1862:

> ...the confronting lines looked into each other's faces at deadly range, less than one hundred yards apart, and they stood as immovable as the painted heroes in a battle-piece....Out in the sunlight, in the dying daylight, and under the stars, they stood, and though they could not advance, they could not retire. There was some discipline in this, but there was much more of true valor.

Rigid linear tactics had been appropriate for 18th- and early 19th-century armies equipped with smoothbore muskets that fired a round ball accurately only at close range, but most Union and Confederate soldiers carried muskets with rifled bores that fired conical bullets called minié balls, the range of which measured hundreds of yards. While the average soldier could fire no more than three rounds per minute with his muzzle-loading musket, rapid-firing, breech-loading rifles and carbines were coming into widespread use, and artillery was more lethal and mobile than ever before.

Advances in military hardware coupled with antiquated tactics led to the virtual annihilation of some units. At Seven Pines, 373 of 632 men in the 6th Alabama fell; at Gettysburg, the 1st Minnesota lost 82 percent of its strength, and 588 of some 850 soldiers in the 26th North Carolina were killed or wounded. On June 18, 1864, at Petersburg, the 1st Maine Heavy Artillery (fighting as infantry) suffered the greatest numerical loss of any regiment, North or South—900 men went into the charge, and only 268 returned.

That the Civil War soldier fought on despite such losses was due to discipline as well as ideology, although that discipline did not come easily. Particularly difficult for volunteers to accept was the enforced respect and obedience due superior officers; after all, many officers had been voted into rank by their troops, who now resented their high-and-mighty ways. When General Philip Kearny reprimanded one of his sergeants caught stealing peaches from an orchard, the soldier snapped, "Who the hell are you?" The volunteers hated being confined to training camp when their families lived nearby, sentry duty appeared foolish to soldiers quartered in Washington or Richmond, and being forced to drill in summer heat seemed senseless and cruel. But First Manassas proved that an army was only as good as its discipline. As early as the second month of war, officers like Major Wilder Dwight of the 2nd Massachusetts recognized the need for military professionalism. "The voluntariness has died out in the volunteer," Dwight wrote. "He finds himself devoted to regular service. A regular he must be made, and the rules and articles of war, in all their arbitrary severity, will not sit lightly upon him."

Given the carefully choreographed, close-order tactics of 19th-century

CAVALRY GUIDON, reenactment

warfare, every soldier had to memorize a complex, often bewildering litany of commands. Training was monotonous and constant. As the disgruntled Union Private Oliver W. Norton recorded:

> The first thing in the morning is drill, then drill, then drill again. Then drill, drill, a little more drill. Then drill, and lastly drill. Between drills, we drill, and sometimes stop to eat a little and have a roll-call.

Despite its "arbitrary severity," such training fostered a sense of regimental pride that inspired units to compete for honors on the battlefield and soldiers to freely offer their lives in defense of their regimental colors.

As the conflict became a war of attrition, however, soldiers could not help but fall prey to increasing cynicism and bitterness. "Oh, this damned rebellion will make brutes of us all, if it is not soon quelled!" wrote Union Lieutenant Frank Haskell after Gettysburg. Following his regiment's decimation at Cold Harbor, Private Lewis Bissell of the 2nd Connecticut Heavy Artillery sent a letter home from "Cold Harbor and Hell." "If there is ever again any rejoicing in this world," he wrote, "it will be when this war is over. One who has never been under fire has no idea of war." Veterans saw all too clearly that a soldier must kill or be killed. When a Confederate captain voiced regret that he could not prevent his men from shooting a conspicuously gallant Union officer, Stonewall Jackson reproved him, "No, Captain. The men are right. Kill the brave ones. They lead on the others."

If in its chivalric pretensions and its outmoded tactics the Civil War was the last of the old wars, it was also the first of the new, one in which the concept of "total war" gained reluctant acceptance in the minds of generals and privates alike. The purposeful destruction of civilian property was a strategy from which neither side was immune. Even before the emergence of Grant and Sherman, Union Colonel Strong Vincent wrote:

> We must fight them more vindictively, or we shall be foiled at every step. We must desolate the country as we pass through it, and not leave the trace of a doubtful friend or foe behind us; make them believe that we are in earnest, terribly in earnest...that the life of every man, yea, of every weak woman or helpless child in the entire South, is of no value whatever compared with the integrity of the Union.

However, the overwhelming testimony of the men who fought the Civil War clearly indicates that Vincent's view was atypical. For all the bloodshed, Victorian concepts of glory and honor remained to the end. Nowhere were they more evident than in the surrender ceremony at Appomattox as the victorious Union soldiers offered a salute to their enemy.

When veterans wrote their memoirs, most emphasized the war's chivalry, not

MONUMENT TO MAJOR GUSTAVUS LIGHTFOOT, 12th Missouri, Vicksburg National Military Park, Mississippi

its butchery. Today this may seem like a perverse glorification of war, but to judge these men on 20th-century terms is to do them a disservice. The sincerity of their beliefs and the intensity of their words had nothing to do with glorification and everything to do with the strength of their ideals.

No veteran more exemplified nor more eloquently expressed those ideals than Joshua Lawrence Chamberlain. A professor of religion and modern languages at Bowdoin College before the war, he was a contemplative man who became a consummate soldier. As colonel of the 20th Maine, he played an important role in the Union victory at Gettysburg. His conspicuous bravery on a score of battle-fields won him the Medal of Honor and promotion to the rank of general, and, like many soldiers, he paid a price for his gallantry.

On June 18, 1864, during an assault on the Confederate defenses of Petersburg, Chamberlain was struck by a bullet that passed through his body from hip to hip. Bones were fractured, muscles severed, his bladder torn. Given the state of 19th-century medicine, the wound was tantamount to a death sentence, and the surgeons told him as much. But within five months he was once more at the front. Unable to walk a hundred yards, unable to mount a horse without indescribable pain, Chamberlain saw the war through to the end when his brigade accepted the formal Confederate surrender at Appomattox.

Chamberlain suffered from his injury the rest of his life. The wound never healed, and he underwent half a dozen major operations that left him bedridden for weeks at a time. His death at the age of 85, after a career that included active involvement in veterans' affairs and service as both governor of Maine and president of Bowdoin College, came as a direct result of the bullet fired 50 years earlier.

In his numerous postwar writings and speeches, Chamberlain sought to understand the Civil War, and though he was a living casualty of the conflict, he came to endow it with a sublime, essentially religious profundity. Ironic as it may seem, Chamberlain took issue with General Sherman's famous statement that war was "all hell." While he agreed that the killing and destruction were demonic, Chamberlain was convinced that the virtues engendered by the experience of war far outweighed its vices. He believed that selfless devotion to principle, fortitude in the presence of pain, hope in the face of adversity, and, above all, the Christian ideal of sacrifice for the sake of others transcended cruelty and hatred and conferred on the war's survivors an almost mystical sense of brotherhood. "What wonder that men who have passed through such things together," Chamberlain wrote, "should be wrought upon by that strange power of a common suffering which so divinely passes into the power of a common love."

Most Civil War veterans shared Chamberlain's views, and if they could not romanticize the war's horror, they willingly exalted its deeds of valor and encouraged its elevation to epic stature. Robert Stiles, a Yale graduate who fought for

UNION SOLDIER'S GRAVE, Starr King Cemetery, Jefferson, New Hampshire

SERGEANT, 73rd New York

the Confederacy, told a gathering of former comrades, "If there is any part of your life where you should have been, and did what you should have done, it is the great Olympiad of '61 to '65. What have you felt or looked on since that is not pitifully small in comparison?" Many veterans felt an obligation to perpetuate the memory of those years. "In our youth our hearts were touched with fire," said Oliver Wendell Holmes, Jr., a thrice-wounded veteran who went on to brilliant service as a justice of the United States Supreme Court. "We have seen with our own eyes, above and beyond the gold fields, the snowy heights of honor, and it is for us to bear the report to those who come after us."

Rather than fostering sectional differences, Southern veneration of the "Lost Cause" was intrinsically linked to national reconciliation. "It is all the better that the war was fought, even though our cause went down in defeat," Colonel N. E. Harris remarked at a 1912 reunion of the United Confederate Veterans. "The struggle has left a heritage of brave deeds, a history of heroic endurance, of fidelity to country and home and fireside for the whole American nation, North and South, to cherish."

In 1887, when the survivors of Pickett's Confederate division and their former opponents of the Philadelphia Brigade met at Gettysburg, both groups spontaneously extended hands across the stone wall where 24 years earlier Virginians and Pennsylvanians locked in combat. This symbolic handshake became a ritual at future Gettysburg reunions, one that was carried down through the years till the last veterans were too infirm to participate.

It was largely due to the efforts of veterans that a number of the war's great fields were purchased and set aside for future generations. Monuments of granite and bronze were erected as tangible reminders of the courage with which Union and Confederate regiments marched to sacrifice. Standing on the battlefield of Chattanooga, former Confederate General William Bate expressed the common hope of all veterans when he said, "These monuments shall last...and through all the coming years shall inspire our remotest descendants with that loyalty to conviction which these fields illustrate."

Those monuments and those fields still inspire. The monuments are worn with age, the fields are tranquil, but one can sense the distant thunder of the guns. And to stand upon ground consecrated with the blood of thousands who cherished their beliefs more strongly than life itself is to touch the heart of this nation.

Brian C. Pohanka
Leesburg, Virginia

CONFEDERATE CAVALRYMEN, reenactment

CANNON, Gettysburg National Military Park, Pennsylvania

No chemistry of frost or rain, no overlaying mould of the season's recurrent life and death, can ever separate from the soil of these consecrated fields the life-blood so deeply commingled and incorporate here. Ever henceforth under the rolling suns, when these hills are touched to splendor with the morning light, or smile a farewell to the lingering day, the flush that broods upon them shall be rich with a strange and crimson tone, — not of the earth, nor yet of the sky, but mediator and hostage between the two.

But these monuments are not to commemorate the dead alone. Death was but the divine acceptance of life freely offered by every one. Service was the central fact.

General Joshua Lawrence Chamberlain
Gettysburg, October 3, 1889

FORT SUMTER, 1861

FORT SUMTER, South Carolina. At 4:30 A.M. on April 12, 1861, the salvo of a 10-inch mortar arched over the waters of Charleston Harbor and exploded above Fort Sumter as decades of increasing tension between the North and South erupted in armed conflict. Thousands of jubilant Charlestonians thronged the town's docks and rooftops to enjoy the fiery spectacle. Sumter's Federal garrison capitulated two days later, and the flag of the Confederacy was raised above its ramparts.

CONFEDERATE INFANTRYMAN

*A*t half past four Captain James, from Fort Johnston, pulled his lanyard; the great mortar belched forth, a bright flash, and the shell went curving over in a kind of semi-circle, the lit fuse trailing behind, showing a glimmering light, like the wings of a fire fly, bursting over the silent old Sumter. This was the signal gun that unchained the great bull-dogs of war....

Private D. Augustus Dickert
South Carolina Militia
Fort Sumter

FORT MOULTRIE, South Carolina. From Fort Moultrie Southern artillerymen fired shell after shell into Fort Sumter just under a mile distant, but neither side suffered a fatality. Federal forces had occupied Fort Moultrie on December 10, 1860, when South Carolina became the first state to secede from the Union. Six days later Major Robert Anderson decided the fort was indefensible and evacuated his tiny garrison to Sumter under cover of night. Ironically, during the Revolutionary War, Anderson's father had helped defend Fort Moultrie against the British.

MARCHING UNION TROOPS, reenactment

The quick, vigorous step, in rhythmical cadence to the music, the fife and drum, the massive swing, as though every man was actually a part of every other man; the glistening of bayonets like a long ribbon of polished steel, interspersed with the stirring effects of those historic flags, in countless numbers, made a picture impressive beyond the power of description. A picture of the ages. How glad I am to have looked upon it....I can still see that soul-thrilling column, that massive swing, those flaunting colors, that sheen of burnished steel! Majestic! Incomparable!! Glorious!!!

Lieutenant Frederick L. Hitchcock
132nd Pennsylvania

STATUE OF GENERAL THOMAS J. JACKSON, Manassas National Battlefield Park, Virginia. The armies' first great clash came on July 21, 1861, in the First Battle of Manassas, or Bull Run as it was known in the North. One of the war's best-known legends was inspired by reports that Confederate Brigadier General Barnard E. Bee steadied his troops with the exclamation, "There stands Jackson like a stone wall! Rally behind the Virginians!" Although some officers asserted that Bee, who died the next day, had meant to criticize Jackson, the former Virginia Military Institute professor was honored as "Stonewall" from then on.

CONFEDERATE SOLDIERS, Washington Artillery of New Orleans, 1861

UNION ARTILLERY POSITION, Manassas. The encounter was replete with blunders on both sides. Most recruits had received only rudimentary training, and many regimental commanders were equally new at their task. The fact that some Confederate units wore blue uniforms and several Union regiments were outfitted in gray added to the confusion. The battle's turning point came when the blueclad 33rd Virginia Regiment overran two batteries of Federal cannon; Brigadier General Irvin McDowell's chief of artillery had mistaken them for Union troops.

RHODE ISLAND VOLUNTEERS, 1861

*T*he order was now given to charge bayonets....and we passed forward with a cheer, not in a very regular line but each one striving to be foremost. But in passing over the stubble or pasture field we discovered it bore an abundant crop of blackberries, and being famished with hunger and our throats parched with thirst, the temptation was too strong to be resisted, the men stopped with one accord and the charging line of battle resolved itself into a crowd of blackberry pickers. Officers swore or exhorted, according to their different principles, and presently succeeded in getting the line to move on. Still, whenever an unusually attractive bush was passed over, we reached down without stopping and stripped off berries, leaves and briers, which we crammed into our mouths; for days afterwards I was occupied extracting the thorns from the palms of my hands.

Private McHenry Howard
1st Maryland, C.S.A.
First Manassas

CONFEDERATE TROOPS, reenactment. After the First Battle of Manassas, the Northern press temporarily ceased its belligerent cry of "On to Richmond," but the triumphant Confederates failed to pursue the retreating Union army to Washington, where a conclusive victory might have been quickly won. Both sides had fought with unexpected ferocity; the war was clearly going to be a long and costly struggle.

CONFEDERATE MONUMENT, Shiloh National Military Park, Tennessee. The first great battle
in the western theater began on April 6, 1862, when Confederate General Albert Sidney Johnston
launched a dawn attack on Major General U.S. Grant's forces encamped near Shiloh Church.
The unsuspecting Grant was absent, and his soldiers stared in disbelief as the Southern troops
bore down upon them, shouting the rebel yell, a high-pitched *ki-yi-yi* reminiscent of an Indian
war whoop.

PITTSBURG LANDING, Tennessee River. By late afternoon of April 6, thousands of demoralized Union soldiers had retreated to Pittsburg Landing. The survivors of shattered regiments huddled on the riverbank or milled about in confusion, unwilling to reenter the conflict despite their officers' entreaties. But on the surrounding bluffs other Yankee troops fought on, bolstered by artillery fire and salvos from the U.S. gunboats *Tyler* and *Lexington*.

. . . We heard the voice of a wounded man crying: "Boys! boys!" Thinking it might possibly be one of our men we went to him. He first begged for a drink of water, which I gave him out of my canteen. . . . His name was John Burns, Company B, Fourth Ohio Regiment. . . . He had a small Bible in his hand with his thumb resting inside on the fourteenth chapter of St. John. His thumb being bloody it made a bloody spot on this chapter. He desired that this Bible be sent to his mother, showing where he last read.

Joe T. Williams
21st Alabama
Shiloh

UNION TENT HOSPITAL SITE, Shiloh. Shiloh was the war's bloodiest battle to date, costing more than 13,000 Union and 10,000 Confederate casualties. Neither army had sufficient medical staff and supplies. Although surgeons labored day and night in their improvised operating rooms, many wounded died before receiving proper medical attention, and a number of the injured, abandoned where they fell, received no care at all.

MANSE GEORGE CABIN, Shiloh. Farmer Manse George's house was caught in the vortex of the first day's fight as Grant's forces tried to check the waves of Confederate attackers. The 3rd Iowa and a battery of Michigan artillery were driven from their position near the cabin by Colonel William Stephens's brigade of Tennessee and Kentucky troops. But the Rebels paid dearly for their success; General Johnston fell mortally wounded.

(*Above and facing*) FORT PULASKI, Georgia. In April 1862, Fort Pulaski, a Confederate stronghold on Tybee Island, guarding the port of Savannah, was pounded into submission by a 30-hour bombardment from besieging Federal forces. While only a dozen members of the garrison were killed or wounded, long-range, rifled Union cannon extensively damaged the fort, which had been built in 1830 with the help of a 23-year-old army engineer named Robert E. Lee.

UNION ARTILLERY POSITION, Malvern Hill, Richmond National Battlefield Park, Virginia

We never think of being beaten here. I think our cause is brighter now than it has ever been since the commencement of the war. Those glorious victories of old Stonewall have struck terror in the Yankee hearts.

William McKnight
17th Virginia
Near Richmond, June 1862

STATUE OF GENERAL ROBERT EDWARD LEE, Charlottesville, Virginia. On June 1, 1862, Lee assumed command of the forces defending Richmond, the Confederate capital, replacing General Joseph E. Johnston who had been seriously wounded the previous day in the Battle of Seven Pines. While Lee was a highly regarded officer in the prewar army, nothing so far had distinguished his Civil War career. Nevertheless he would prove equal to his task when the newly christened Army of Northern Virginia confronted Major General George B. McClellan's Army of the Potomac, now within 10 miles of Richmond.

PENNSYLVANIA MONUMENT, Cold Harbor National Cemetery, Virginia. Again and again in the bloody week of fighting known as the Seven Days, Lee hurled his troops upon McClellan's in desperate attempts to drive the Federal forces from Richmond and destroy them. He succeeded only in keeping McClellan on the defensive, forcing him to withdraw to his supply base on the James River. On June 27, the retreating Union soldiers passed through Cold Harbor en route to the Battle of Gaines' Mill; many would fight there again in 1864.

UNION HORSE ARTILLERY OFFICERS IN WINTER CAMP, Brandy Station, Virginia, 1864

*O*ccasionally *a* woman *passes camp and it is a three days wonder. But women only serve to remind me of you and our separation and I don't care to see them. I do not have the* bad thoughts *about them that some do. The only woman I care to see is you my* loved one.

Sergeant Edwin H. Fay
Mississippi Cavalry

CONFEDERATE OFFICER AND CIVILIANS, reenactment. With the exception of runaway slaves, or "contrabands," who flocked to the Union armies, many soldiers had only limited contact with civilians. Leave of absence was usually a privilege reserved for officers, and a number of homesick volunteers chose to desert rather than to endure separation from their families.

UNION CAVALRY, reenactment. During the war's first two years, the Federal mounted arm was outmatched by its Confederate counterpart. Most Northern troopers were either city-born or farmers more familiar with draft horses than with Thoroughbreds, and so lacked equestrian skills. Under the aggressive leadership of Major General James Ewell Brown "Jeb" Stuart, Southern horsemen literally rode rings around McClellan's army and easily frustrated the Yankee cavalrymen's attempts at scouting and reconnaissance.

CEDAR MOUNTAIN BATTLEFIELD, near Culpeper, Virginia. On August 9, 1862, the Federal corps of General Nathaniel P. Banks, a former speaker of the House of Representatives, who had been outmaneuvered by Jackson in the Shenandoah Valley earlier that year, clashed with him again in the shadow of Cedar Mountain. In heat that rose above 100°, the Union troops temporarily routed the Stonewall Brigade. But Jackson rallied his men, and when A.P. Hill's reinforcements arrived, he managed to regain lost ground.

*O*ne beautiful night during these terrible days I was sitting in the moonlight, looking up into the heavens so beautiful and calm—while everything around us which men controlled was full of evil and death—when the bands of the contending armies began to play.…One band struck up "Home Sweet Home," and was followed by others until all the bands of both sides joined in. Then the soldiers of both sides began to sing it, each gathering inspiration from the others, until all swelled the chorus, and the spirit of war was hushed as all hearts thought of the loved ones at home.

Captain Edward H. McDonald
11th Virginia Cavalry

(Above and facing) CONFEDERATE ENCAMPMENT, reenactment. A young Union officer named Oliver Wendell Holmes, Jr. once complained that the war was an "organized bore." Both Union and Confederate soldiers spent far more hours in the mundane chores of drill and fatigue duty than they did in battle. What free time they were allowed was passed in letter writing, card playing, singing, joking, or simply dozing in canvas tents.

*W*e had evidence of what the Fifth Texas had done in the
ghastly, horrifying spectacle that met our eyes as we looked at
the hill-side in our rear, nearly an acre of which was covered
with the killed and wounded Zouaves, the variegated colors of
whose gaudy uniforms gave the scene, when looked at from a
distance, the appearance of a Texas hill-side when carpeted in
the spring by wild flowers of many hues and tints.

> J.B. Polley
> Hood's Texas Brigade
> Second Manassas

(Above and facing) 5TH NEW YORK ZOUAVES, reenactment. The 5th New York Volunteer Infantry was one of many Civil War regiments — most of them Northern — clad in colorful regalia adopted from the French Zouaves, elite colonial troops who modeled their uniforms on North African garb. Superbly drilled and ably led, the 5th paid a heavy price for their valor while trying to stem the attack of Longstreet's Confederate corps in the Second Battle of Manassas. In less than 10 minutes, 297 of the regiment's 490 men fell, 117 of them dead or dying.

STATUE OF MAJOR GENERAL PHILIP KEARNY, Arlington National Cemetery, Virginia. On September 1, 1862, two days after the Confederate victory at Second Manassas, Jackson confronted retreating Union forces in the Battle of Chantilly. In the middle of a thunderstorm, the Federals fought him to a standstill, but lost their most colorful, reckless division commander when one-armed General Phil Kearny mistakenly rode into Confederate lines and was shot dead from his horse.

CONFEDERATE ARTILLERY PIECE, reenactment. A notable day in the history of Southern artillery came at Manassas on August 30, 1862. Behind the bank of an unfinished railroad, Stonewall Jackson's infantrymen were hard pressed by a Federal assault until massed batteries of Confederate cannon opened fire and the exploding shells and hissing shrapnel staggered the Union flank.

NEW YORK MONUMENT, Antietam National Battlefield, Maryland

At sunrise when the red haze of early morning was mantling the eastern skies, all nature arrayed in gorgeous beauty seemed standing on tip-toe silently waiting the coming contest.

John W. Stevens
5th Texas
Antietam

HARPERS FERRY, West Virginia. After Second Manassas, Lee embarked on an ambitious campaign; he invaded Northern territory, crossing the Potomac River into Maryland. On September 15, 1862, Jackson hemmed in the Federal garrison occupying Harpers Ferry at the strategically vital confluence of the Potomac and Shenandoah Rivers, and shelled the Union troops into submission. Some 12,000 Yankees laid down their arms—the war's largest Union surrender.

MONUMENTS TO THE 128TH AND 137TH PENNSYLVANIA, Cornfield Avenue, Antietam. On September 17, 1862, the Army of Northern Virginia fought McClellan's numerically superior Army of the Potomac near Antietam Creek, which flowed past the village of Sharpsburg. The Union assault began at sunrise, and soon a battle of charge and countercharge raged through farmer David Miller's cornfield. When the 128th Pennsylvania advanced into the trampled field from the cover of the East Woods, their colonel and 117 men were mowed down in minutes; the 1st Texas Infantry endured losses of 82 percent.

BURNSIDE'S BRIDGE, 1862. McClellan's final offensive was launched against Lee's right, where a handful of Georgia riflemen held a limestone bridge spanning Antietam Creek. Throughout the day Major General Ambrose Burnside's Federal troops made repeated efforts to cross the bridge, though the stream itself was fordable in several places. Finally a charge by the 51st Pennsylvania and 51st New York carried the span, and Burnside began to drive the outnumbered Confederates back to Sharpsburg.

SOUTHWEST FROM THE NORTH WOODS, Antietam. Both sides claimed Antietam as a victory, though in truth it was a tactical draw. Lee countered his opponent's every move and still held his position. McClellan failed to coordinate his attacks and refused to commit reserves that might have won the day. But Lee could ill afford another such bloodletting and decided to call off his invasion of the North; in that sense Antietam was undeniably a strategic victory for the Union.

UNION SOLDIER, with Colt revolving rifle

Hastily emptying our muskets into their lines, we fled back through the cornfield....Oh, how I ran! Or tried to run, through the high corn, for my heavy belt and cartridge box and musket kept me back to half my speed. I was afraid of being struck in the back, and I frequently turned half around in running, so as to avoid if possible so disgraceful a wound.

Private John E. Dooley
1st Virginia
Antietam

132ND PENNSYLVANIA MONUMENT, Bloody Lane, Antietam. Failing to break Lee's northern flank at the cornfield and Dunker Church, McClellan struck at the Confederate center. But when the Union 2nd Corps crested a low ridge, they met the musketry of Rebel soldiers in a sunken farm road below. Among the scores who fell were many officers and color bearers; it was late afternoon before the Confederate line was flanked and overrun, turning the road into a corpse-strewn "bloody lane."

DUNKER CHURCH, Antietam

DUNKER CHURCH, 1862. As Lee continued to fend off McClellan's attacks, the battle swept through the West Woods and past the church of a pacifist Baptist sect known as the Dunkers. Canister—tin cylinders filled with iron balls—from Confederate guns posted near the church tore great gaps through the Federal lines, but the Southern artillerists did not go unscathed. More than 26,000 soldiers fell at Antietam, making it the bloodiest single day in American history.

CONFEDERATE CAVALRYMAN

It was a dreadful scene, a veritable field of blood. The dead and dying lay as thick over it as harvest sheaves. The pitiable cries for water and appeals for help were much more horrible to listen to than the deadliest sounds of battle. Silent were the dead, and motionless. But here and there were raised stiffened arms; heads made a last effort to lift themselves from the ground; prayers were mingled with oaths, the oaths of delirium; men were wriggling over the earth; and midnight hid all distinction between the blue and the grey. My horse trembled under me in terror, looking down at the ground, sniffing the scent of blood, stepping falteringly as a horse will over or by the side of human flesh; afraid to stand still, hesitating to go on, his animal instinct shuddering at this cruel human misery.

> *Lieutenant Henry Kyd Douglas, C.S.A.*
> *Antietam*

POTOMAC RIVER AND VIRGINIA, from Maryland. As Lee's army retreated back across the Potomac River, McClellan encamped to rest his battered forces. His refusal to immediately pursue and engage the Confederates ultimately cost him his command. Despite his disappointment with McClellan's performance, President Lincoln decided the time was opportune to issue an Emancipation Proclamation, freeing slaves held in Southern territory and vesting the Union cause with a potent ideological foundation.

Coffee is made in large camp kettles holding several gallons, and it would astonish you to see what quantities of it the men drink. Strong coffee, liberally sweetened, is the favorite beverage here, and it goes well and does good when one is just off guard duty these cold mornings. I will not say it is the only beverage drank here, for there is a sulter's shop here, where cider and beer are sold.

Private Benjamin W. Jones
Surry Light Artillery, C.S.A.

(*Above and facing*) INFANTRY ENCAMPMENT, reenactment. An infantryman's daily routine was prescribed by army regulations. Immediately after daybreak the regimental fifes and drums played reveille, and soldiers filed into line for morning roll call. When Surgeon's Call was sounded shortly afterwards, ailing men went to the surgeon's tent to be examined, hoping for an official excuse from duty for the day. Meanwhile the rest tidied their tents and company streets, performed their morning ablutions, and cooked their standard rations of hardtack, fried salt pork, and strong black coffee.

UNION SENTRIES, reenactment. Guard duty was an unpleasant but inevitable part of soldier life, as every regiment was required to maintain a picket line 24 hours a day, no matter how inclement the weather. The sentinels' deportment was strictly defined and rigidly enforced. Anyone attempting to pass through the picket line was challenged with the watchword or countersign of the day; muskets were never allowed to touch the ground, nor was the sentinel permitted to sit or even lean against a tree. The penalty for falling asleep on guard duty was death.

CONFEDERATE TROOPS, reenactment. Because no Southern commanders in the west performed as ably as Lee in the east, the war's western theater devastated Confederate hopes.
In August of 1862, Major General Braxton Bragg led an invasion of Union-held Kentucky that
reached its high-water mark at Perryville on October 8. A favorite of President Jefferson Davis
but an officer of dubious ability, Bragg retreated from the field after a drawn battle that cost
him some 3,400 men.

Shells came direct and oblique, and dropped down from above. Shells enfiladed the lines, burst in front, in rear, above and behind; shells everywhere. A blizzard of shot, shell and fire.

The lines passed on steadily. The gaps made were quickly closed. The colors often kissed the ground, but were quickly snatched from dead hands and held aloft again by others, who soon in their turn bit the dust. The regimental commanders marched out far in advance of their commands and they too fell rapidly, but others ran to take their places....

But on, still onward, the line pressed steadily. The men dropping in twos, in threes, in groups. No cheers or wild hurrahs as they moved towards the foe. They were not there to fight, only to die.

Colonel St. Clair A. Mulholland
116th Pennsylvania
Fredericksburg

(Above and facing) FREDERICKSBURG NATIONAL CEMETERY, Fredericksburg, Virginia. On December 13, 1862, General Ambrose Burnside, an affable but mediocre officer best known for the bushy side whiskers that gave the English language a new word, committed his forces to a series of costly attacks against Lee's formidable defenses on Marye's Heights, a ridge overlooking the Rappahannock River and Fredericksburg. Time and again the blue ranks advanced, only to dissolve in a hurricane of fire. Nearly 13,000 Yankee troops fell before night put a stop to the slaughter.

LIEUTENANT HORATIO D. JARVES, 24th Massachusetts

IN MEMORIAM
RICHARD ROWLAND KIRKLAND
CO. G, 2ND SOUTH CAROLINA VOLUNTEERS

KIRKLAND MONUMENT, Fredericksburg and Spotsylvania County Battlefields Memorial National Military Park, Virginia. The war that pitted American against American, neighbor against neighbor, and brother against brother was not lacking in gestures of kindness and mercy. The day following the Battle of Fredericksburg, a young Confederate named Richard Rowland Kirkland passed among the thousands of wounded Union soldiers who lay groaning on the frozen slopes, dispensing water and words of encouragement. Kirkland, who would later die in action, was dubbed "The Angel of Marye's Heights."

Strong men wept for him, with a sense of loss and desolation....His veterans mourned as men do rarely—dumb and still before this terrible fatality; and General Lee, who knew his incomparable value more than all other men, exclaimed, with tears in his eyes, "He is better off than I am. He lost his left arm, but I have lost my right!"

Captain John Esten Cooke, C.S.A.

STATUE OF GENERAL THOMAS JONATHAN JACKSON, Charlottesville, Virginia. In the spring of 1863, Major General Joseph Hooker embarked on a skillfully planned campaign to surround and destroy Lee's forces west of Fredericksburg. But at Chancellorsville on May 2, the Confederates took the initiative. Lee split his forces, launching Stonewall Jackson in a successful surprise attack on Hooker's flank and rear. That evening Jackson was shot by Confederates who mistook him and his staff for a Yankee cavalry detachment. Seven days after Jackson's shattered arm was amputated, he died of shock and pneumonia.

RUINS OF CHANCELLOR HOUSE. For all his careful strategy and superior numbers, by the morning of May 3, Hooker's Army of the Potomac was on the defensive. Despite the disheartening loss of Jackson, Lee's forces fought well and by afternoon had wedged Hooker's troops into the fields surrounding Union headquarters at the Chancellor House. Riddled with shrapnel, the building caught fire; Hooker himself was injured when a porch column against which he was leaning was struck by a Rebel shell.

CONFEDERATE CAVALRYMAN, reenactment

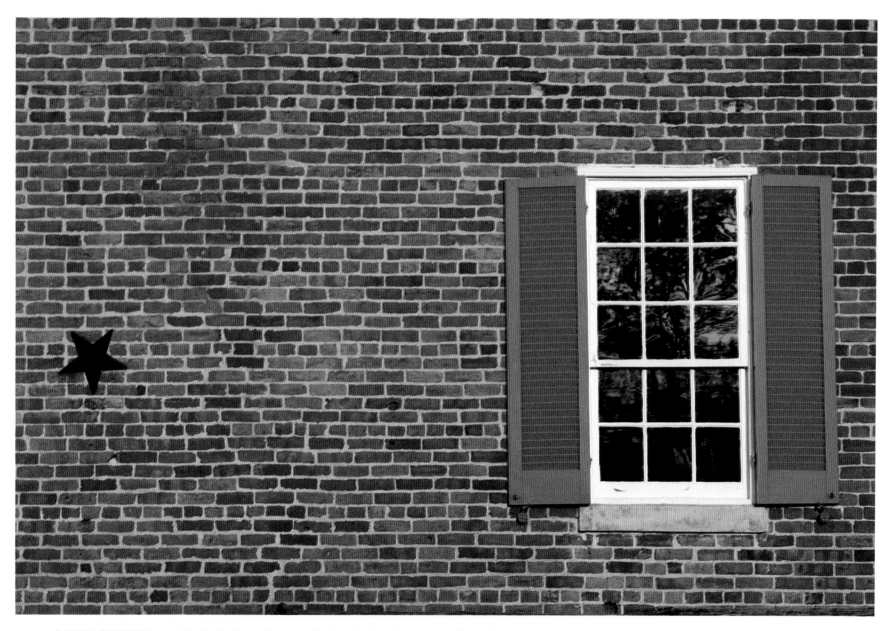

SALEM CHURCH, near Fredericksburg, Virginia. Having broken through the Confederate troops guarding the Rappahannock River at Fredericksburg, Major General John Sedgwick's 6th Corps marched west to join Hooker's embattled forces at Chancellorsville on the afternoon of May 3. Only the Confederate brigade of Brigadier General Cadmus M. Wilcox stood in the way of Sedgwick's 20,000 men, but at little Salem Church the outnumbered Alabamians slowed the Union advance long enough for Lee to dispatch reinforcements who turned the tide of battle against the North.

WISCONSIN STATE MEMORIAL, Vicksburg National Military Park, Mississippi

As the smoke was slightly lifted by the gentle May breeze, one lone soldier advanced, bravely bearing the flag towards the breast works. At least a hundred men took deliberate aim at him, and fired at point-blank range, but he never faltered. Stumbling over the bodies of his fallen comrades, he continued to advance. Suddenly, as if with one impulse, every Confederate soldier within sight of the Union color bearer seemed to be seized with the idea that the man ought not to be shot down like a dog. A hundred men dropped their guns at the same time; each of them seized his nearest neighbor by the arm and yelled to him: "Don't shoot at that man again. He is too brave to be killed that way...." As soon as they all understood one another, a hundred old hats and caps went up into the air, their wearers yelling at the top of their voices: "Come on, you brave Yank, come on!"

Charles Evans
2nd Texas
Vicksburg

BATTLE MONUMENT, United States Military Academy, West Point, New York. The Mississippi River fed men and supplies to the heart of the Confederacy; from the beginning of the war control of the river was a vital part of the Union's overall strategy. The most formidable Confederate stronghold on the river was Vicksburg, Mississippi, and in November 1862, General Grant made the first moves in a campaign that would culminate eight months later with the conquest of that Southern bastion.

UNION EARTHWORKS, Vicksburg. On May 19, 1863, having outmaneuvered his opponents and brought his 35,000-man army to the outskirts of Vicksburg, Grant launched an attack on the earthen fortifications ringing the town. The assault was bloodily repulsed; another charge on May 22 fared no better. Grant determined to lay siege to the town and starve the 30,000 Confederate defenders into surrender. The Yankee soldiers began to dig in and within a week had erected more than 10 miles of trenches, forts, and redoubts.

UNION SERGEANT

What an awful eight minutes that was, we having to lay there not allowed to fire a single shot at the enemy who was sending to eternity by scores our brave boys' souls! Oh, how my heart palpitated! It seemed to thump the ground (I lay on my face) as hard as the enemy's bullets. The sweat from off my face ran in a stream from the tip ends of my whiskers. God only knows all that passed through my mind. Twice I exclaimed aloud that my comrades might hear "My God, why don't they order us to charge," and then I thought perhaps all of our officers were killed and there was no one to order us forward. I thought of dear friends, of home and of heaven, but never wished, as did some who were near me that, I had never attempted to charge, and, indeed, wished that I had not become a soldier. Some who were wounded groaned and shrieked, others were calm and resigned. Generally those that were the slightest wounded shrieked the loudest, thinking they were wounded the worst.

Captain Charles E. Wilcox
33rd Illinois
Vicksburg

WISCONSIN STATE MEMORIAL, Vicksburg. To divert Confederate attention from his march on
Vicksburg, Grant sent a former music teacher named Colonel Benjamin H. Grierson with 1,700 horse
soldiers on an ambitious raid deep behind Confederate lines. Grierson's forces covered 600 miles in
16 days, took 500 prisoners, destroyed over 50 miles of railroad track and telegraph lines, and burned
countless tons of enemy supplies, losing fewer than 30 men themselves. Not only did the raid have
its desired strategic effect, it also gave an immeasurable boost to the morale of the Union cavalry.

USS *CAIRO*. In the campaign against Vicksburg, ironclad gunboats of the U.S. Navy played a significant role, which the Confederates tried to counter with torpedoes. On December 12, 1862, when the USS *Cairo* sank beneath the muddy waters of the Yazoo River, a tributary of the Mississippi, it was the first of some 40 Union ships lost to these primitive mines. In *Cairo*'s case the torpedo was a submerged gunpowder-filled keg triggered by a hand line held by a Confederate on the river bank. Less reliable types of torpedoes were detonated by contact with the vessel.

CONFEDERATE MONUMENT, Port Gibson, Mississippi. On April 30, 1863, Grant's army crossed the Mississippi south of Vicksburg, and the following day an outnumbered Confederate division commanded by Brigadier General John S. Bowen tried to slow the Union advance near Port Gibson. The battle cost the Confederates 832 men killed, wounded, and missing; the dead included Brigadier General Edward Tracy, instantly killed at the beginning of the fight. The Union victory left Grant free to drive north, isolating the Confederate garrison in Vicksburg.

CONFEDERATE SOLDIER, reenactment

UNION SIEGE BATTERY, Vicksburg. As the seige of Vicksburg went on, Lieutenant General John C. Pemberton realized that a continued defense was impossible. Supplies were virtually exhausted and the soldiers weakened by hunger. Half of Pemberton's forces had been killed or wounded. The plight of the town's civilian population was little better; Union shelling forced many women and children to shelter in underground bombproofs and caves, and some subsisted on a diet of mule meat and rats. On July 4, 1863, Pemberton agreed to Grant's demand for an unconditional surrender.

8TH PENNSYLVANIA CAVALRY MONUMENT, Gettysburg National Military Park, Pennsylvania

*A*nother spring shall green these trampled slopes, and flowers, planted by unseen hands, shall bloom upon these graves; another autumn and the yellow harvest shall ripen there....In another decade of years, in another century, or age, we hope that the Union, by the same means, may repose in a secure peace, and bloom in a higher civilization.

Lieutenant Frank A. Haskell
2nd Corps, Army of the Potomac
Gettysburg

FIRST SERGEANT HORACE EDGERLY, 12th New Hampshire

The hoarse and indistinguishable order of commanding officers, the screaming and bursting of shells, canister and shrapnel with their swishing sound as they tore through the struggling masses of humanity, the death screams of wounded animals, the groans of their human companions, wounded and dying and trampled under foot by hurrying batteries, riderless horses and the moving lines of battle, all combined an indescribable roar of discordant elements — in fact, a perfect hell on earth, never, perhaps, to be equalled, certainly not to be surpassed, nor ever be forgotten in a man's lifetime. It has never been effaced from my memory, day or night, for fifty years. It was grim-visaged war, with all its unalterable horror, implacable, unyielding, full of sorrow, heart breaks, untold sufferings, wretched longings, doubts and fears.

> *Robert G. Carter*
> *22nd Massachusetts*
> *Gettysburg*

EMMITSBURG ROAD AND CEMETERY RIDGE, Gettysburg. In June 1863, the Army of Northern Virginia, 90,000 strong, again crossed the Potomac River into Union territory and headed north. This time Lee's forces were bound for Pennsylvania and the lush farmland of the Cumberland Valley. Under General Hooker the Army of the Potomac began a furious march to intercept and confront the Confederate invasion, but three days before the inevitable collision, Hooker was replaced by Major General George G. Meade. On July 1, the two armies stumbled into action near the little town of Gettysburg, and the greatest conflict of the war began.

CONFEDERATE DEAD, near Plum Run, Gettysburg, 1863. The first day of fighting belonged to Lee's Confederates; thousands of Union troops were driven through the town in confusion but rallied on high ground known as Cemetery Hill and Cemetery Ridge. That evening the bulk of Meade's army arrived on the field, and during an even bloodier struggle on July 2, managed to fight the Confederates to a standstill. Hundreds of men fell in the boggy, boulder-strewn valley of Plum Run, a place known thereafter as "The Valley of Death."

4TH MAINE INFANTRY MONUMENT, near Devil's Den, Gettysburg. On the afternoon of the second day's fight, the onslaught of General Longstreet's Confederates pushed the Federal 3rd Corps from the Emmitsburg road to Cemetery Ridge. Some of the heaviest fighting took place amidst an outcropping of massive boulders called Devil's Den; there, while defending a Union battery, the 4th Maine fought bayonet to bayonet with the 44th Alabama Regiment. One out of every three men in the 4th Maine fell.

UNION BATTLE LINE, reenactment. Both armies at Gettysburg were composed almost entirely of veteran regiments, units which had lost two-thirds or more of their men to bullets or disease. The survivors were well-disciplined and toughened by their previous service—lean, muscular, and sunbrowned. Their uniforms were patched and faded, but their weapons were in good working order, and their morale high. They fought with the standard Napoleonic tactics of the day: elbow to elbow, rank behind rank, firing into their foe at ranges that often closed to less than 50 yards.

THE PEACH ORCHARD, Gettysburg. In defiance of Meade's instructions, Major General Daniel Sickles advanced his 3rd Corps to high ground along the Emmitsburg road, a gentle slope crested by orderly rows of peach trees. Longstreet's attack smashed this "peach orchard salient" and sent Sickles's divisions reeling back toward the main Union line on Cemetery Ridge. The oncoming Confederates stepped over the bodies sprawled among the shattered fruit trees, realigned their ranks, then surged forward screaming the rebel yell.

CONFEDERATE INFANTRYMAN

With a withering and deadly fire pouring in upon us from every direction, it seemed that the regiment was doomed to destruction. While one man was shot in the face, his right-hand or left-hand comrade was shot in the side or back. Some were struck simultaneously with two or three balls from different directions. Captains Hill and Park suggested that I should order a retreat; but this seemed impracticable. My dead and wounded were then nearly as great in number as those still on duty. They literally covered the ground. The blood stood in puddles in some places on the rocks; the ground was soaked with the blood of as brave men as ever fell on the red field of battle.

Colonel William C. Oates
15th Alabama
Gettysburg

LITTLE ROUND TOP, Gettysburg. Gettysburg, the great turning point of the war, was itself a battle of turning points, of crises met by subordinate officers who often performed independently of their commanders. Brigadier General Gouverneur Kemble Warren found to his shock that the crucial promontory of Little Round Top, which dominated Meade's left flank, was unoccupied by Union troops. On his own initiative, Warren hastened regiments to the crest in time to meet the charging Confederate Texas Brigade. The Southerners were driven back, and the Union flank was saved.

1ST INDEPENDENT COMPANY MONUMENT, Massachusetts Sharpshooters, Gettysburg

69TH PENNSYLVANIA INFANTRY MONUMENT, Cemetery Ridge, Gettysburg. On the afternoon of July 3, Lee made a last effort to break the Union center on Cemetery Ridge. In the wake of an artillery bombardment, three divisions of Confederate troops swept forward. Major General George E. Pickett's Virginians managed to pierce the Union line near a stone wall and copse of trees. But again the blue ranks, including the largely Irish 69th Pennsylvania, held firm, and Pickett's men recoiled in defeat. It was the Confederate high-water mark, the end of Lee's hopes for victory at Gettysburg.

COLOR GUARD, 33rd New York

Halt! Break ranks! In camp at last, but such a camp. On the wet, damp ground to lie—no blankets, no oil-cloths, no wagons, no cooking utensils and nothing to cook, nothing to eat. Commissary inefficient, badly managed, disorganized .... "Hello, boys, here's where the cavalry fed their horses and here are the grains of corn left by the horses." We gladly picked them up, parched and ate them with a relish. Hunger is a great sauce.

Major William A. Smith
14th North Carolina

LINE OF "A" OR WEDGE TENTS, reenactment. As the war continued, veteran soldiers learned to make do with less. To lighten their load on the march, the men threw away anything that was expendable and some things, such as tents and overcoats, that were not. Instead of heavy knapsacks, many soldiers carried only a rolled blanket, a rubber ground cloth, and a canvas shelter half, which buttoned to a comrade's half to form a small "dog" or "pup" tent. The more spacious and bulkier wedge tents were generally reserved for new regiments and garrison troops.

MEMORIAL TO COLONEL ROBERT GOULD SHAW AND THE 54TH MASSACHUSETTS
REGIMENT, Boston, Massachusetts. In 1863, the Federal government finally heeded the calls of
abolitionist and Negro leaders to allow free blacks to enlist in the army. Many politicians and military
men doubted blacks' abilities as soldiers, but the heroism of the black 54th Massachusetts dispelled
this misconception. On July 18, 1863, led by Colonel Robert Gould Shaw, a white Bostonian, the 54th
spearheaded a futile but valiant charge on Fort Wagner, one of Charleston's defenses. Colonel Shaw
and 271 of his men fell in the attack.

RUINS OF FORT SUMTER. The Union had symbolic as well as military reasons for laying siege to Charleston; South Carolinians fired the first shot of the war. But the city's defenders repeatedly thwarted Union assaults from land and sea and defied the daily rain of Union shells. Of all the Confederate positions at Charleston, none was more symbolic or proved more unconquerable than the battered Fort Sumter.

UNION FIRST SERGEANT

*A*bout 11 A.M. we were ordered forward, facing west, and very soon encountered a veritable hailstorm of grapeshot and Minie balls from the enemy....but we had learned something in battle experience; so we fell flat to the ground until the Yankees emptied their guns, when we rose up and with the Rebel yell, in which the brigade had become proficient, we charged the second line of breastworks and drove the enemy pell-mell through the woods....

> *John T. Goodrich*
> *3rd Tennessee*
> *Chickamauga*

FLORIDA STATE MONUMENT, Chickamauga and Chattanooga National Military Park, Georgia. On the second day of the Battle of Chickamauga, the Union Army of the Cumberland led by Major General William S. Rosecrans, a popular but poor field commander, was struck a stunning blow by Bragg's Army of the Tennessee. A confusion in orders caused a gap in the Union line at the very point where Longstreet's Confederate corps advanced to attack. The Federal brigades crumbled, then fled in panic; even Rosecrans and his staff were swept along in the rout.

95

13TH MICHIGAN REGIMENTAL MONUMENT, Chickamauga. The 13th Michigan Regiment, part of Colonel George Buell's brigade, was heavily engaged in the fighting on September 19, 1863. In the next day's even bloodier conflict, the Michiganders were caught in the middle of Longstreet's Confederate onslaught. ''The shock came like an avalanche,'' Buell reported, and the 13th fared no better than the brigade's other regiments. Over 100 of the regiment fell, and its ranks scattered in confusion.

BROTHERTON CABIN, Chickamauga. The Confederates poured across the fields of the Brotherton farm, killing or capturing all who tried to stop them. Union cannon belched forth canister that ripped through the Rebel ranks like huge shotgun shells. Nothing slowed them until they reached the slopes of Horseshoe Ridge, where Union Major General George Thomas made a determined rearguard stand despite Rosecrans's absence and earned the appellation "Rock of Chickamauga."

UNION SUPPLY BOATS, Chattanooga, Tennessee, 1863. In October 1863, Grant took charge of the Union forces defending the supply base at Chattanooga. Bragg's Confederate army besieged the Yankee troops from high ground overlooking the town. But Grant was able to feed and equip his command, thanks in large part to the military transports and steamers that plied the Tennessee River. In November the Federal commander lashed out at his opponents in a series of battles that sealed the fate of the Confederate army in the west.

CONFEDERATE ARTILLERY EMPLACEMENT, Lookout Mountain, Tennessee. The positions held by the Confederates near Chattanooga seemed impregnable: rugged slopes dominated by the naked cliffs of Lookout Mountain. This did not deter Grant, and on November 24, 1863, the Union troops fought to the summit in a "battle above the clouds." The next day Grant launched an advance on Confederate outposts below Missionary Ridge. Flushed with success, the Yankee infantrymen pressed on, ignoring orders to halt, and clawed their way to the crest of the ridge. Bragg's army was forced to retreat.

Soon the gates of hell on earth were closed on us. Many a poor soul never passed out again — except to be carried to the dead house.

> John I. Faller
> 7th Pennsylvania
> Andersonville

CONFEDERATE MONUMENT, Johnson's Island, Ohio. The fate of military prisoners in the Civil War was a hard one, particularly after the system of man-for-man exchanges broke down midway in the conflict. Although the North was far better equipped than the South to feed, clothe, and house captives, neither side could control the spread of disease encouraged by overcrowding and cold, damp weather. Thirty thousand Confederates perished in prison compounds like the one on Lake Erie's windswept Johnson's Island.

UNION PRISONERS OF WAR, Andersonville, Georgia, c. 1864. No prison camp, North or South, was more feared than Andersonville. The very name evoked horror, and many a Yankee soldier preferred death on the battlefield to incarceration in the disease-ridden stockade. At one time Andersonville held more than 33,000 men, of whom an average of 30 died every day. All of the prisoners were emaciated and dressed in rags, and most were without shelter; the only source of drinking water doubled as the stockade's latrine.

THE WILDERNESS, near Spotsylvania, Virginia

We moved on through the interminable forest and endless night. The winds tossed the leafless branches of the trees, seeming to moan and shudder. There was none of the usual hilarity and enthusiasm that attend the breaking of camp. This army has so often been led forward only to be driven back, torn and bleeding, that it has almost lost hope. Though Lee's ranks are decimated and our own have been largely augmented, and we hope for a short and decisive campaign, yet none have the courage to prophesy anything but defeat.

> *John W. Haley*
> *17th Maine*
> *With Grant on the spring campaign of 1864*

PRIVATE THOMAS A. BATES, 6th Kentucky, U.S.A.

*S*o many whom I know have been killed, that it makes it seem but a short step from this to the next world. You can have no idea with what perfect indifference every one here regards life. You hear the same conviviality, the same jokes, songs and mirth, when we are just on the eve of an engagement as in camp.

Major Peter Vredenburgh
14th New Jersey
After Spotsylvania

UNION SOLDIER'S GRAVE, Tyringham Cemetery, Tyringham, Massachusetts. In the spring of 1864, General Grant headed east to Virginia. Newly appointed general in chief of the Union armies, Grant intended to destroy Lee's Army of Northern Virginia once and for all. On May 5, he caught up with Lee in the tangled thickets of the Virginia Wilderness, a landscape that made tactical coordination and regimental alignment nearly impossible. For two days men slaughtered one another amidst the flames of underbrush ignited by musketry. Scores of wounded perished in the fires.

15TH NEW JERSEY MONUMENT, Spotsylvania. Although he was unable to vanquish Lee in the Wilderness, Grant was determined to press his offensive. The bloodied Yankee forces continued southward and again collided with Lee's Rebels, this time near Spotsylvania Court House. The second great battle in less than a week cost both sides dearly. Grant's men hurled themselves upon improvised Confederate defenses of earth and fence rails, fighting with bayonets and gun butts, and firing into the enemies' faces at pointblank range.

CONFEDERATE TROOPS, reenactment. The fight at Spotsylvania on May 12 was the most vicious hand-to-hand struggle of the war. At dawn the Federal 2nd Corps came shouting out of the mist and surged over a crucial Confederate salient called the Mule Shoe. Lee ordered a counterattack that plugged the hole in the Confederate line. At one terrible "Bloody Angle" of the defenses, the opposing lines fought continuously for 10 hours. The hail of lead cut down whole trees, and some regiments suffered casualties of 50 percent or more.

UNION HOSPITAL, Fredericksburg, Virginia. In one month of fighting—at the Wilderness, Spotsylvania, and Cold Harbor—Grant's army lost 50,000 men killed, wounded, and captured. The Union's hospitals overflowed. The soft lead of .58-caliber minié balls shattered bones, making amputations common. Anaesthesia and morphine were widely used, and many medical officers skillfully carried out complex surgical procedures. Still, since most doctors only vaguely understood the need for medical sterilization, thousands of wounded succumbed to postoperative infections.

STATUE OF MAJOR GENERAL JOHN SEDGWICK, West Point, New York. Among Grant's senior officers the proportion of casualties was higher than among common foot soldiers. In the mid-19th century, even generals were expected to be in the midst of battle. On May 9, the Army of the Potomac lost one of its most admired corps commanders when a Confederate sharpshooter picked off "Uncle John" Sedgwick while he inspected the lines of his 6th Corps. Sedgwick had ignored warnings of danger, commenting, "Why, they couldn't hit an elephant at that distance."

(Above and facing) ENCAMPMENT IN THE SHENANDOAH VALLEY, reenactment. The year 1864 brought the war home with a vengeance to the inhabitants of Virginia's Shenandoah Valley. The South needed and the North wanted this fertile "breadbasket of the Confederacy," and three Federal armies vied for control of the Valley with Generals Breckinridge's and Early's Confederate forces. The Union commanders ordered widespread burning of crops, barns, and grist mills, and confiscated horses and cattle. Foraging Yankee soldiers eagerly supplemented their rations with pilfered poultry and livestock.

CONFEDERATE SOLDIERS

Then came a sound more stunning than thunder. It burst directly in my face: lightnings leaped, fire flashed, the earth rocked, the sky whirled round. I stumbled, my gun pitched forward, and I fell upon my knees.... "Hurrah!" I thought, "youth's dream is realized at last. I've got a wound, and am not dead yet."

Cadet John S. Wise
Virginia Military Institute
New Market

CONFEDERATE TROOPS, reenactment. The initial Confederate defense of the Valley culminated in victory at the Battle of New Market on May 15, 1864. That day the teenaged Corps of Cadets from Lexington's Virginia Military Institute charged and captured a disabled Union battery, routing the cannon's defenders. The novices' display of valor helped defeat Major General Franz Sigel's Federal army, but the battle caused only a temporary setback to Union designs in the Valley.

MONUMENT TO MAJOR GENERAL WILLIAM MAHONE, Petersburg National Battlefield, Virginia

*W*e halted in a ravine, as near the rebel works as possible, and the commanding officer of the division addressed the line as follows:

"Boys, I want you to go in there and capture that battery and works. There are but a few 'rebs' in there, and they will run when they see you. We have got batteries posted all around—that you know nothing about—that will assist you. I have no time to lose—you can have the works in ten minutes." (And most of us knew better and some said he was drunk.) "I will be there as soon as you are!"—but [he] remained behind.

Charles Lowell Nightingale
29th Massachusetts
Near Petersburg, June 1864

BOMBPROOF IN FORT SEDGWICK, Petersburg. By June 1864, Grant's troops were stale-mated in a deadly siege at Petersburg. Both sides constructed trenches, earthworks, and forts on a scale unprecedented in the history of warfare. Neither could maneuver to advantage, and the struggle became a duel of sharpshooters who fired at the slightest movement. On July 30, the Federals triggered four tons of powder that had been tunneled beneath the Confederate lines by the 48th Pennsylvania, a regiment whose ranks included many coalminers, but attack-ing Union troops failed to charge past the gaping crater it left.

STATUE OF MAJOR GENERAL U.S. GRANT, Vicksburg. Grant was undeterred by his casualties in the Wilderness Campaign. A realist, utterly indifferent to the trappings and show of 19th-century warfare, Grant was willing to grind Lee's outnumbered forces down through attrition. The Union commander knew that his losses could be replaced, while Lee's could not. Lincoln had instituted a draft in 1863, and substantial bounties tempted other Northerners to enlist.

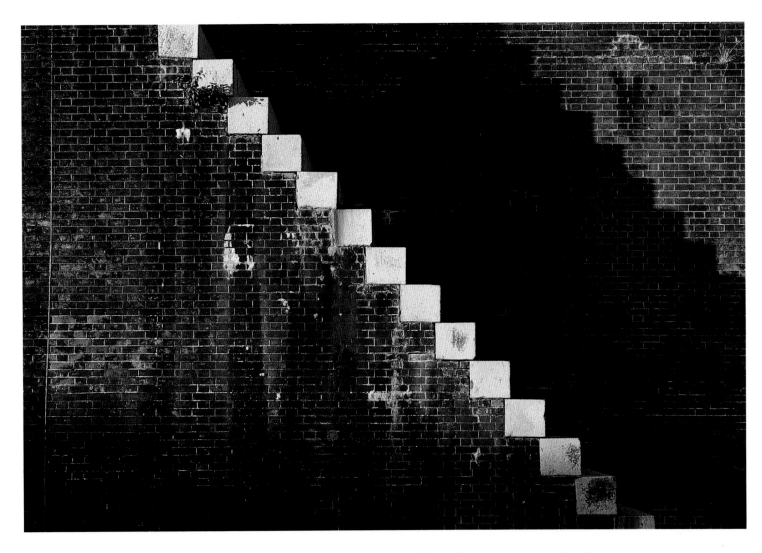

STEPS AT FORT MORGAN, Alabama. At the beginning of August 1864, the Union launched combined naval and land operations against the port of Mobile, one of the Confederacy's last open harbors. Two massive prewar forts, Morgan and Gaines, guarded access from the Gulf of Mexico, while the formidable ironclad CSS *Tennessee* and three Confederate gunboats waited in the bay to engage Admiral David G. Farragut's Federal fleet.

FORT GAINES, Alabama. As the Union 13th Corps laid siege to Fort Gaines by land, Farragut's fleet ran the three-mile gauntlet between the guns of Morgan and Gaines, and confronted Admiral Franklin Buchanan's Confederate vessels in Mobile Bay. The fire from the Rebel forts inflicted little damage on the Union ships, but nearly 100 Yankee sailors were lost when the monitor *Tecumseh* struck a floating torpedo and sank.

FORT MORGAN CITADEL, c. 1864

CASEMATES AT FORT MORGAN. Lashed in the rigging of his flagship, the USS *Hartford*, Admiral Farragut damned the torpedoes, sailed full speed ahead, and won a decisive victory over the Southern fleet. Fort Gaines capitulated soon thereafter, and on August 23, following a bombardment from land and sea, the 400-man garrison of Fort Morgan surrendered.

BENJAMIN HARVEY HILL HOUSE, Athens, Georgia. Built in the 1850s, the elegant Greek revival mansion of engineer John Thomas Grant epitomized a way of life that vanished with the downfall of the Confederacy. By the end of 1864, few Southerners held any illusions about the future of their cause; the Confederate armies were in retreat, and William Tecumseh Sherman was marching through Georgia to the sea, leaving ruin in his wake.

To enter a house and find the feather bed ripped open, the wardrobes ransacked, chests stripped of contents, looking glasses taken from the walls, cooking utensils gone, and all the corn meal and bacon missing, bed quilts stripped from the beds, the last jar of pickles gone, was no uncommon sight, and one to make a soldier blush with indignation. Every effort that could be made was made to check the demoralization of the foragers; but the occupation tended to demoralization, and "the army must be fed, and the Bummers must feed us." Thus we reasoned, but deprecated the means used to bring about the result. Some would discriminate, others would not, and thus the few have caused a great deal of unnecessary suffering.

Lieutenant Charles A. Booth
20th Corps, U.S.A.

CONFEDERATE DEFENSES, Atlanta, 1864. On September 1, following a series of hard-fought battles, Confederate commander John Bell Hood was forced to abandon Atlanta to Sherman's army. Union troops occupied the deserted Rebel earthworks. Then at Sherman's order, they evacuated the civilian population and turned the entire city into a fortified camp. Sherman's harsh measures earned him the undying enmity of Southerners, but those measures hastened the end of the war.

EXPERIMENTAL CONFEDERATE CANNON, Athens, Georgia. During the Civil War countless inventors tried to create deadly new weapons. Many of these, including torpedoes, hand grenades, and machine guns, came into use, but others proved less than practical. The peculiar double-barreled cannon cast at the Confederate foundry in Athens and designed by John Gilleland was intended to simultaneously fire two cannon balls linked by an iron chain. Improper synchronization of the trigger mechanisms caused one barrel to discharge slightly before the other, snapping the links.

CONFEDERATE MEMORIAL, Augusta, Georgia. Statues of Generals W.H.T. Walker and T.R.R. Cobb stand guard over Augusta's memorial to her Confederate soldiers. As the war neared its end, the South was increasingly handicapped by a vacuum in command; 77 of the Confederacy's general officers were killed in action or died of wounds. General Walker was fatally wounded in the Battle of Atlanta, while Cobb, a prominent Georgia lawyer and author, died from wounds received at the Battle of Fredericksburg in December 1862.

CONFEDERATE SOLDIER

One woman, I distinctly remember, with three little pale, starved girls clinging about her, herself barefoot, bareheaded, thinly and miserably clad, seized my arm with a vise-like grip, and begged for the love of God, for just a morsel for her starving children. They had tasted nothing since Sunday morning, and then only a spoonful of dry meal. I gave her the contents of my haversack, and one man in the ranks, a great, rough, swearing fellow, poured into her lap his entire three days' rations of pork and hard bread, thrust a ten dollar greenback, all the money he possessed, into her hand, swearing like a pirate all the while as a means of relief to his overcharged feelings, their intensity being abundantly evident by the tears which coursed rapidly down his cheeks. . . .

Lieutenant Royal B. Prescott
13th New Hampshire
Richmond

RUINS OF GALLEGO MILLS, Richmond, 1865. The Confederacy's final desperate week began with the evacuation of Richmond on the night of April 2, 1865. After nearly 10 months of siege, Lee had at last abandoned Petersburg in the face of massive Union assaults that struck all along his line, opening Richmond to invasion. Warehouses and supply depots were put to the torch so that supplies would not fall into enemy hands, and as the last of the Southern garrison crossed the James River bridges and ascended the heights beyond, they looked back at a city in flames.

APPOMATTOX COURT HOUSE NATIONAL HISTORICAL PARK, Virginia

The spectacle presented on that bright spring morning was one never to be forgotten, and whether looking from the summit of the highland around Appomattox, or from the village itself, it was of surpassing beauty and grandeur. . . . The troops of the Corps, not yet fully deployed, in deep lines, stretching around a vast amphitheater under a bright sun on a carpet of fresh green, and looking over a quiet and apparently untenanted town, and on the lower land beyond, the enemy brought to bay, with their foes before them and behind them. And then what one who was there can forget the emotions inspired, the consciousness that the end was accomplished, and that he had a part in the glory of it?

Captain George M. Laughlin
5th Corps, Army of the Potomac
Appomattox

FEDERAL CANNON, Sayler's Creek Battlefield Historical State Park, Virginia. The Army of Northern Virginia marched west, hoping to link up with General Joseph Johnston's army, which was falling back before Sherman. Lee's soldiers were discouraged and exhausted, and many simply struck off for home. Grant pursued closely, the Union soldiers sensing that victory could not be far off. On April 6, 1865, a third of Lee's force was surrounded and defeated in battle on the banks of Sayler's Creek. Six generals were captured, among them Lee's son Custis.

MCLEAN HOUSE, Appomattox. Following the First Battle of Manassas, Wilmer McLean moved from his homestead near Bull Run to the village of Appomattox, an obscure backwater of the war. But on April 9, 1865, the armies again came to McLean's doorstep. Lee and Grant met inside the parlor of his home to arrange the surrender of the Army of Northern Virginia.

CLOVER HILL TAVERN, Appomattox. The formal surrender of Lee's Army, which came three days after the meeting at McLean's house, was a heart-rending moment for the soldiers of the Confederacy as they stacked their muskets and furled their flags for the last time. Men on both sides wept. Union Brigadier General Joshua Chamberlain, whose brigade accepted the symbolic surrender of arms and colors, ordered his men to salute the passing Southern ranks. At the command of Major General John B. Gordon, the Confederate troops returned the gallant gesture.

The God of battles was against us, and we were defeated, but not dishonored nor disgraced. We returned to homes in ruin, our fortunes gone, and nothing left but honor, pluck, and energy.

James A. Jones
23rd Tennessee

CONFEDERATE SOLDIER, reenactment. Grant's surrender terms were stern but fair, fully in accord with Abraham Lincoln's desire for postwar reconciliation. Grant ordered that rations be distributed to the famished Southerners and permitted soldiers who owned their horses to keep them. The Confederates were quickly paroled, issued passes, and allowed to return to their homes where they faced an uncertain future in a country again united.

SOLDIERS' GRAVES, Arlington National Cemetery

In great deeds something abides. On great fields something stays. Forms change and pass; bodies disappear; but spirits linger, to consecrate ground for the vision-place of souls. And reverent men and women from afar, and generations that know us not and that we know not of, heart-drawn to see where and by whom great things were suffered and done for them, shall come to this deathless field, to ponder and dream; and lo! the shadow of a mighty presence shall wrap them in its bosom, and the power of the vision pass into their souls.

> *General Joshua Lawrence Chamberlain*
> *Gettysburg, October 3, 1889*

Quotation Sources and Permissions
Pages 13 and 135 from "General Chamberlain's Address" by Joshua Lawrence Chamberlain in MAINE AT GETTYSBURG, REPORT OF MAINE COMMISSIONERS PREPARED BY THE EXECUTIVE COMMITTEE, 1898. Page 16 from HISTORY OF KERSHAW'S BRIGADE by D. Augustus Dickert, 1899. Page 18 from WAR FROM THE INSIDE by Frederick L. Hitchcock, 1904. Page 22 from RECOLLECTIONS OF A MARYLAND CONFEDERATE SOLDIER by McHenry Howard. 1914 Reprint. Copyright 1975 Morningside Bookshop. Reprinted by permission of Morningside House, Inc. Page 26 from "Death of a Union Soldier at Shiloh" by Joe T. Williams in *Confederate Veteran* 10 (April 1902). Reprinted by permission. Page 31 from The McKnight Papers, Manuscript in Lloyd House Library. Alexandria Library, Alexandria, Virginia. Reprinted by permission. Page 34 from Fay, Edwin H., "THIS INFERNAL WAR" THE CONFEDERATE LETTERS OF SGT. EDWIN H. FAY. Edited by Bell Irwin Wiley with the Assistance of Lucy E. Fay. Austin: University of Texas Press, 1958. By permission of the publisher. Page 38 from "We Drove Them from the Field" by Edward H. McDonald in *Civil War Times Illustrated* November 1967, reproduced with the permission of Historical Times, Inc. Page 40 from HOOD'S TEXAS BRIGADE by J. B. Polley. 1910 Reprint. Copyright 1976 Morningside Bookshop. Reprinted by permission of Morningside House, Inc. Page 45 from REMINISCENCES OF A CIVIL WAR SOLDIER by John W. Stevens, 1902. Page 50 from Dooley, John E., JOHN DOOLEY CONFEDERATE SOLDIER. Edited by Joseph T. Durkin, S.J. Georgetown: Georgetown University Press, 1945. Reprinted by permission of Georgetown University Press. Page 54 from I RODE WITH STONEWALL by Henry Kyd Douglas. © 1940 The University of North Carolina Press. Reprinted by permission. Page 56 from UNDER THE STARS AND BARS: A HISTORY OF

THE SURRY LIGHT ARTILLERY by Benjamin W. Jones. 1909 Reprint. Copyright 1975 Morningside Bookshop. Reprinted by permission of Morningside House, Inc. Page 60 from THE STORY OF THE 116TH REGIMENT, PENNSYLVANIA INFANTRY by St. Clair A. Mulholland, 1903. Page 64 from STONEWALL JACKSON: A MILITARY BIOGRAPHY by John Esten Cooke, 1866. Page 69 from DEEDS OF VALOR edited by W. F. Beyer and O. F. Keydel, 1906. Page 72 from "With Grant at Vicksburg—From the Civil War Diary of Captain Charles E. Wilcox" edited by Edgar L. Erickson in *Journal of the Illinois State Historical Society* 30 (January 1938). Illinois State Historical Society. Reprinted by permission. Page 79 from HASKELL OF GETTYSBURG edited by Frank L. Byrne and Andrew T. Weaver. Copyright 1970 State Historical Society of Wisconsin. Reprinted by permission. Page 80 from FOUR BROTHERS IN BLUE by Robert G. Carter. 1913 Reprint. Copyright 1978 University of Texas Press. Reprinted by permission. Page 86 from "Colonel Oates Almost Captures Little Round Top" by William C. Oates in THE WAR BETWEEN THE UNION AND THE CONFEDERACY AND ITS LOST OPPORTUNITIES, WITH A HISTORY OF THE 15TH ALABAMA REGIMENT AND THE FORTY-EIGHT BATTLES IN WHICH IT WAS ENGAGED, 1905. Page 90 from THE ANSON GUARDS COMPANY C, FOURTEENTH REGIMENT NORTH CAROLINA VOLUNTEERS 1861-1865 by W. A. Smith, 1914. Page 94 from "Gregg's Brigade in the Battle of Chickamauga" by John T. Goodrich in *Confederate Veteran* 22 (June 1914). Reprinted by permission. Page 100 from DEAR FOLKS AT HOME: THE CIVIL WAR LETTERS OF LEO W. AND JOHN I. FALLER WITH AN ACCOUNT OF ANDERSONVILLE edited by Milton E. Flower. Copyright 1963 Cumberland County Historical Society. Reprinted by permission. Page 103 from Haley, John W. THE REBEL YELL AND THE YANKEE HURRAH, Ruth Silliker, Editor. Camden, Maine:

Down East Books, 1985. Reprinted by permission. Page 104 from Martin, David G. (ed.), THE MONOCACY REGIMENT, A COMMEMORATIVE HISTORY OF THE FOURTEENTH NEW JERSEY INFANTRY IN THE CIVIL WAR, 1862-1865. Hightstown, N. J.: Longstreet House, 1987. Reprinted by permission. Page 112 from THE END OF AN ERA by John S. Wise, 1902. Page 115 from Charles Lowell Nightingale Letters. Houghton Library, Harvard University, Cambridge, Massachusetts. By permission of the Houghton Library. Page 122 from "An Inventory of the Bummer" by Charles A. Booth in THE STAR CORPS; OR, NOTES OF AN ARMY CHAPLAIN, DURING SHERMAN'S FAMOUS "MARCH TO THE SEA" by G. S. Bradley, 1865. Page 126 from "The Capture of Richmond" by R. B. Prescott in CIVIL WAR PAPERS... MASSACHUSETTS COMMANDERY, MILITARY ORDER OF THE LOYAL LEGION OF THE UNITED STATES, 1900. Page 129 from "Memories of Appomattox" by George M. Laughlin in UNDER THE MALTESE CROSS, 1910. Page 132 from "About the Battle of Shiloh" by James A. Jones in *Confederate Veteran* 7 (December 1899). Reprinted by permission.

Archival Photography Credits
Pages 2, 20, 34, 72, 90, and 104 from the U.S. Army Military History Institute. Pages 5, 10, 16, 22, 50, 54, 80, 86, 94, 112, and 126 from the Collection of Kean E. Wilcox. Pages 14, 48, 62, 65, 82, 93, and 120 from the Massachusetts Commandery, Military Order of the Loyal Legion and the U. S. Army Military History Institute. Pages 53, 74, 98, 101, 108, 116, 123, and 127 from the Library of Congress.

Reenactment Scenes
Pages 7, 11, 56, 57, 58, 59, 66, 76, 110, and 133 photographed in Perryville, Kentucky. Pages 18, 35, 36, 38, 39, 40, 41, 43, and 136 photographed at Cedar Mountain, Virginia. Pages 23, 84, 91, 107, 111, and 113 photographed in New Market, Virginia.